Sing-Along Praise

Praise

Piggyback Songs about God's Love

by Anita Reith Stohs

Illustrated by Michelle Dorenkamp

CONCORDIA PUBLISHING HOUSE · SAINT LOUIS

To Miriam Elizabeth,

for whom a place is waiting in the heavenly choirs.

Exodus 15:19–21

Copyright © 1999 Concordia Publishing House
3558 S. Jefferson Avenue, St. Louis, MO 63118-3968
Manufactured in the United States of America

4   5   6   7   8   9   10   11   10   09   08   07   06   05

Contents

A Word from the Author

Music is a special gift of God to His children. "Piggyback" songs—songs with new words to familiar melodies—offer unique opportunities for God's children to celebrate music and "sing to the Lord a new song."

The piggyback songs in this book come out of years of using music with children, from preschool through eighth grade. It was while working with children living in the inner city and those with developmental disabilities that I found piggyback songs, with their emphasis upon simple words and tunes, to be especially effective teaching aids for reaching children with the Gospel.

The use of familiar tunes and simple, repetitious words offers an effective avenue for teaching basic Christian truths, as well as words of Bible passages. Such songs can be used for openings and closings, as well as lesson review and application.

Adapt these songs to fit your own teaching situation, or better yet, use them as a springboard for writing your own piggyback songs with children.

The piggyback songs in this book were written to proclaim the saving grace and love of God in Christ Jesus. May God's Holy Spirit guide you as you use these songs to communicate this Good News to the children you teach.

Anita Reith Stohs

Mary and the Angel

Melody: *Reuben and Rachel*

Mary, Mary, look beside you.
There's an angel standing there!
It is Gabriel, sent from heaven
With Good News for you to hear.

"Mary, Mary, don't be frightened.
God is with you, favored one.
You will have a little baby,
Jesus Christ, God's own dear Son."

"How can this be?" Mary wondered.
"I've not married anyone."
"God can do all things," said Gabriel.
"The baby will be God's own Son."

"As you say," then Mary answered,
"As God says, so let it be."
We join Mary in her praises;
Jesus came for you and me:

"My soul magnifies the Lord now;
And my soul finds joy in Him.
He has done great wonders for me.
Holy, holy, be His name."

Jesus Is Coming

Melody: *Christmas Is Coming*

Jesus is coming,
    your loud hosannas sing!
Light the Advent candles
    for your Savior King.

With love and forgiveness,
    into our world He comes.
Welcome Him with joy
    into your hearts and homes.

Here We Come

Melody: *Here We Come A-Caroling*

Here we come with songs of joy
   unto Emmanuel.
Of His saving love for all,
   we now will sing and tell.
Hope and peace come to you.
Joy and love be with you too.
And may Christ find a place to live
   within your heart today.
May He find a place to live
   within your heart.

O Come, Little Children

Melody: *O Come, Little Children*

O come, little children,
   and welcome your King.
To Jesus, your Savior,
   loud praises now sing.
He comes to forgive you
   and save you from sin.
To Jesus, your Savior,
   loud praises now sing.

Come, Dear Lord

Melody: *Row, Row, Row Your Boat*

Come, come, come, dear Lord,
Fill my heart today.
Make it now Your dwelling place.
And bless me with Your grace.

O Come, Emmanuel

Melody: *The Farmer in the Dell*

O come, Emmanuel,
O come, Emmanuel.
Come and save your people now.
O come, Emmanuel.

Now let us sing with joy,
Now let us sing with joy.
Jesus came to save us all.
Now let us sing with joy.

O come, Emmanuel,
O come, Emmanuel.
Live within our hearts we pray.
O come, Emmanuel.

Light a Candle

Melody: *Jimmy Crack Corn*

Light a candle for hope today,
Light a candle for hope today,
Light a candle for hope today.
Advent time is here.

Light a candle for peace today …

Light a candle for joy today …

Light a candle for love today …

Light a candle for Christ today,
Light a candle for Christ today,
Light a candle for Christ today.
Christmastime has come.

Sing a new stanza each week in Advent.
Sing the last stanza at Christmas.

Ring the Bells

Melody: *Jingle Bells*

Ring the bells,
Ring the bells,
Ring the bells today.
Jesus came,
Jesus came
For us on Christmas Day.

Ring the bells,
Ring the bells,
Ring the bells today.
Jesus came,
Jesus came
To take our sins away.

*Have the children shake jingle bells as
they sing.*

Christ Was Born in Bethlehem

Melody: *Michael, Row the Boat Ashore*

Christ was born in Bethlehem.
Alleluia!
Born to save us from our sin.
Alleluia!

Songs of joy the angels sang.
Alleluia!
To see Jesus, shepherds ran.
Alleluia!

Every girl and every boy.
Alleluia!
Join us in our song of joy.
Alleluia!

Mary and Joseph

Melody: *Mulberry Bush*

Mary and Joseph went to Bethlehem,
Bethlehem, Bethlehem.
Mary and Joseph went to Bethlehem,
Riding on a donkey.

There was no room left for them,
Left for them, left for them.
There was no room left for them,
Except a little stable.

In that stable Christ was born,
Christ was born, Christ was born.
In that stable Christ was born.
Jesus Christ was born.

Angels sang of Jesus' birth,
Jesus' birth, Jesus' birth.
Angels sang of Jesus' birth.
"Glory to God above."

"Glory, glory!" now we sing,
Now we sing, now we sing.
"Glory, glory!" now we sing
To Jesus Christ, our King.

Joy to the World

Melody: *Skip to My Lou*

Joy to the world, the Lord has come.
Joy to the world, the Lord has come.
Joy to the world, the Lord has come
To save us from our sin.

Joy to the world, the Lord has come.
Joy to the world, the Lord has come.
Joy to the world, the Lord has come.
Glory now we sing.

In a Manger

Melody: *Little Cabin in the Wood*

In a manger Jesus lay
On a little bed of hay.
Shepherds hurried there to see
What had come to be.
What a wonder! What a sight!
Jesus, Lord of heaven bright
As a baby now had come.
To save everyone.

The Angels and the Shepherds

Melody: *Jingle Bells*

"Gloria! Gloria!"
Choirs of angels sing.
"Born today in Bethlehem
Is Christ, your Savior-King."

"Let us go! Let us go!"
Happy shepherds said.
"Let us see the baby there
Inside His manger-bed."

Worship Him, worship Him.
Sing His praise today.
Celebrate the Savior's birth
Now on Christmas Day.

Spread the news, spread the news,
Every girl and boy.
Jesus came to save us all;
Share the news with joy.

Divide into two groups. Have the first group sing stanza 1 and the second sing stanza 2. Repeat with stanzas 3 and 4.

Look in the Sky

Melody: *Up on the Housetop*

"Look in the sky!" the Wise Men say.
   Point up.
"See the star that leads the way.
We will follow it to the King;
   Walk in place.
Gifts to give Him let us bring."

Bumpety bump! Bumpety bump!
   Go up and down.
Riding on the camel's hump.
Over the desert sand they ride,
   Go up and down.
Till they reach the Savior's side.

Lord, as You Have Promised

Melody: *Battle Hymn of the Republic*

Lord, as You have promised,
Let your servant go in peace.
My eyes have seen salvation from
Your hand for everyone.
A light for all the Gentiles,
And the glory of Israel—
The Promised One has come.

Refrain:

Glory, glory! Hallelujah!
Glory, glory! Hallelujah!
Glory, glory! Hallelujah!
The Promised One has come.

Simeon's Song

Melody: *Where, Oh, Where Has My Little Dog Gone?*

To those who walked
In the dark night of sin,
A light from heaven has come.
The light of salvation,
The light of God's love.
Christ Jesus, our true Light has come.

The Wise Men Followed the Star

Melody: *The Bear Went over the Mountain*

The Wise Men followed a bright star.
> *Point to star.*

The Wise Men followed a bright star.
The Wise Men followed a bright star
To find the newborn King.

Chorus:
To find the newborn King,
To find the newborn King.

The Wise Men rode on their camels.
> *Pretend to ride camel.*

The Wise Men rode on their camels.
The Wise Men rode on their camels
To find the newborn King.

Chorus:
To find the newborn King.
To find the newborn King.

The Wise Men followed the bright star.
> *Point to star.*

The Wise Men followed the bright star.
The Wise Men followed the bright star
Until they found their King.

Chorus:
Until they found their King.
Until they found their King.

The Wise Men knelt down and worshiped.
> *Kneel down.*

The Wise Men knelt down and worshiped.
The Wise Men knelt down and worshiped
Jesus, their newborn King.

Chorus:
Jesus, their newborn King,
Jesus, their newborn King.

We too can join them and worship.
> *Fold hands.*

We too can join them and worship.
We too can join them and worship
Jesus, our Savior King.

Chorus:
Jesus, our Savior King.
Jesus, our Savior King.
We too would join them and worship
Jesus, our Savior King.

Wise Men Saw a Shining Star

Melody: *Jack and Jill*

Wise Men saw a shining star.
And followed from afar.
To Bethlehem they came to bring
Their gifts to give the King.

Lamb of God

Melody: *Shenandoah*

O Lamb of God
Who takes away
The sin of all the world.
O Lamb of God,
Have mercy on us.
O Lamb of God, to You we pray,
Grant to us Your peace.

Everybody Needs a Savior

Melody: *London Bridge*

Everybody needs a Savior,
Needs a Savior, needs a Savior.
Everybody needs a Savior.
Yes, we do now!

Jesus came to save us all,
Save us all, save us all.
Jesus came to save us all.
Jesus loves us!

Jesus Suffered

Melody: *Clementine*

Jesus suffered,
Jesus suffered,
Jesus suffered on the cross.
For our sins He suffered gladly.
On the cross
He died for us.

O, dear Savior,
O, dear Savior,
O, dear Savior, You have died
In our place to give us heaven.
Thank You, Jesus
For Your love.

Jesus Died

Melody: *Standing in the Need of Prayer*

Jesus died,
Jesus died,
Jesus died for us.
Died for us upon the cross.
Jesus died,
Jesus died,
Jesus died for us,
Died for us upon the cross.

Jesus rose,
Jesus rose,
Jesus rose for us.
Rose so we can live with Him.
Jesus rose,
Jesus rose,
Jesus rose for us.
Rose so we can live with Him.

Jesus lives,
Jesus lives,
Jesus lives for us.
Lives for us eternally.
Jesus lives,
Jesus lives,
Jesus lives for us.
Lives for us eternally.

On the Cross of Calvary

Melody: *Jesus Loves Me*

On the cross of Calvary
Jesus died for you and me.
In our place He suffered there
To save God's children everywhere.
My Savior died,
My Savior died,
My Savior died.
He died for you and me.

Lord, Have Mercy

Melody: *Kum Ba Yah*

Oh, have mercy, Lord,
On us now.
Oh, have mercy, Lord,
On us now.
Oh, have mercy, Lord,
On us now.
And grant us Your peace, Lord.

Palm Sunday

Sing Hosanna

Melody: *Are You Sleeping?*

Sing hosanna, sing hosanna,
To the King, to the King.
Riding on a donkey,
Riding on a donkey,
Jesus comes, Jesus comes.

Ho-Ho-Hosanna

Melody: *Row, Row, Row Your Boat*

Ho-ho-sanna.
Hosanna now we sing.
Wave your palms and join the praise
Unto the King of Kings.

Oh, the Lord Rode on a Donkey

Melody: *Oh! Susanna*

Oh, the Lord rode on a donkey
Into Jerusalem.
"Hosanna, Son of Da-vid!"
The people cried to Him.

Refrain:
Ho-ho-sanna, Hosanna now we sing,
For our Savior, Jesus Christ has come,
Our great and mighty King.

Oh, the Lord went to the temple then
Into Jerusalem.
"Hosanna, Son of Da-vid"
The children cried to Him.

Refrain:
Ho-ho-sanna, Hosanna now we sing,
For our Savior, Jesus Christ has come,
Our great and mighty King.

Jesus Rose for You and Me

Melody: *Jesus Loves Me*

Jesus rose for you and me.
"Alleluia" let us sing.
Someday we will live with Him.
"Alleluia" let us sing.
Sing, alleluia!
Sing, alleluia!
Sing, alleluia!
He rose for you and me.

The Lord Arose

Melody: *The Lord Is Great*

The Lord arose.
Let everybody sing,
A-a-a-al-le-lu-ia.

The Savior lives.
Let everybody sing,
A-a-a-al-le-lu-ia.

Jesus Has Risen from the Dead

Melody: *John Jacob Jingleheimer Schmidt*

Jesus has risen from the dead.
He lives for me.
Wherever I may go.
He's with me there, I know.
For my Jesus has risen from the dead.
Hosanna! Alleluia!

Jesus has risen from the dead.
Alleluia!
Together we can shout,
And spread the news about.
For my Jesus has risen from the dead.
Hosanna! Alleluia!

Jesus Appears to Mary

Melody: *Where, Oh, Where Has My Little Dog Gone?*

"Where, oh, where has my Jesus gone?
Look down sadly.
Oh, where," thought Mary, "is He?
For His tomb is open
and He is not there.
Oh, where, oh, where, can He be?

Oh, look up, Mary, your Jesus is there.
Look up happily.
Listen to what He will say.
Do not be afraid,
for He calls you by name.
Your Jesus rose on this day.

Then Mary hurried to share
the Good News
Run in place.
That Jesus rose from the dead.
And just like Mary we share
the Good News
That Jesus rose as He said.

Oh, come and join in our glad
hymn of praise,
Clap hands.
Sing Alleluia today.
For our Jesus was dead,
but now lives again,
Sing Alleluia today.

Jesus Rose on Easter Day

Melody: *Jimmy Crack Corn*

Jesus rose on Easter Day,
Jesus rose on Easter Day,
Jesus rose on Easter Day,
We can sing and shout hooray!

My Lord for Us Has Risen

Melody: *My Hat It Has Three Corners*

The Lord is now arisen,
Arisen is our Lord.
For if He was not risen,
We would not rise with Him.

Now sing we alleluia,
Alleluia now we sing.
The Lord for us has risen,
And we will rise with Him.

Praises Let Us Sing

Melody: *Hickory, Dickory, Dock*

Praises now let us sing
Unto our Savior King.
Our Lord arose
On Easter day!
Praises now let us sing.

Jesus Rose for Us

Melody: *Father Abraham*

Jesus rose for us on Easter Day,
Jesus rose for us on Easter.
If we believe in Him
We'll never die,
So let's all praise the Lord!
Al-le-lu-ia! Al-le-lu-ia!
Amen.

*Repeat three times, increasing speed
and adding an additional "Alleluia" line
each time. End by singing "Amen."*

Come and Go with Me

Melody: *Come and Go with Me*

Come and go with me
To the open tomb,
To the open tomb,
To the open tomb.
Come and go with me
To the open tomb.
See that Jesus lives.

Early Easter Day,
Jesus rose again,
Jesus rose again,
Jesus rose again.
Early Easter Day,
Jesus rose again;
Rose for you and me.

We will live forever,
In our Father's house,
In our Father's house,
In our Father's house.
We will live forever,
In our Father's house,
Because Jesus lives.

Alleluia! sing,
Jesus is alive,
Jesus is alive,
Jesus is alive,
Alleluia! sing,
Jesus is alive,
Praise the Lord with joy.

I Know That Jesus Has Died to Save Me

Melody: *I Have Decided to Follow Jesus*

I know that Jesus has died to save me.
I know that Jesus has died to save me.
I know that Jesus has died to save me.
He loves me so. He loves me so.

I know that Jesus has risen for me.
I know that Jesus has risen for me.
I know that Jesus has risen for me.
He loves me so. He loves me so.

I'll live in heaven forever with Him.
I'll live in heaven forever with Him.
I'll live in heaven forever with Him.
He loves me so. He loves me so.

Jesus Died upon the Cross

Melody: *Skip to My Lou*

Jesus died upon the cross,
Jesus died upon the cross,
Jesus died upon the cross,
To take away our sin.

Jesus rose on Easter Day,
Jesus rose on Easter Day,
Jesus rose on Easter Day,
That we might live with Him.

To Emmaus, Two Men Walked

Melody: *The Happy Wanderer*
      (*I Love to Go a' Wandering*)

To Emmaus, two men walked
The first Easter Day.
And as they walked,
The Lord joined them
And talked along the way.
"Stay with us, stay with us.
Stay with us," the two men said.
"Stay with us, stay with us.
Stay with us," the two men said.

Jesus came and ate with them.
As He broke the bread
They realized He was the Lord,
Arisen as He'd said.
Jesus rose, Jesus rose,
Jesus rose just as He said.
Jesus rose, Jesus rose,
Jesus rose just as He said.

Jesus comes and walks with us
As we go on life's way.
And through His Word He talks to us,
He hears us when we pray.
Jesus comes, Jesus comes,
Jesus comes with us each day.
Jesus comes, Jesus comes,
Jesus comes with us each day.

Ascension

Go into All the World

Melody: *Go in and out the Window*

Go into all the world,
Go into all the world,
Go into all the world,
With news of Jesus' love.

Jesus Went up into Heaven

Melody: *Twinkle, Twinkle, Little Star*

Jesus went up into heaven.
Someday He will come again.
Up above the sky He's King
There we'll go to live with Him.
Jesus went up into heaven.
One day He will come again.

Our Savior Ascended

Melody: *On Top of Old Smokey*

As Jesus ascended
Up into the sky,
The clouds came and hid Him
From everyone's eye.

And as the disciples
Looked up after Him.
They saw that two angels
Were standing by them.

"He's gone back to heaven,"
The angels told them.
"And Jesus will come back
The same way again."

Lord, help us tell others
Of Your saving love.
And help us to lead them
To Your home above.

Pentecost

On This Day

Melody: *Jesus Loves Me*

On this day of Pentecost
Came God's Spirit from above.
Spirit, come today we pray,
Fill our hearts with love and faith.
Come, Holy Spirit,
Come, Holy Spirit,
Come, Holy Spirit,
Come fill our hearts we pray.

Fruit of the Spirit

Melody: *Mulberry Bush*

The fruit of the Spirit is love, joy,
    and peace,
Patience, and kindness,
    and goodness too,
Faithfulness, and self-control—
All gifts of the Holy Spirit.

The Holy Spirit Song

Melody: *B-I-N-G-O*

When Jesus was baptized by John,
The Holy Spirit, came.
Holy Spirit, come,
Holy Spirit, come,
Holy Spirit, come
Into our lives today.

At Pentecost, with flames of fire,
The Holy Spirit came.
Holy Spirit, come,
Holy Spirit, come,
Holy Spirit, come
Into our lives today.

Holy Spirit, Come Today

Melody: *Mary Had a Little Lamb*

Holy Spirit, come today,
Come today, come today.
Holy Spirit, come today,
Come and fill my heart, I pray.

Fill my heart with Your good gifts,
Your good gifts, Your good gifts;
Fill my heart with Your good gifts
Come and fill my heart, I pray.

Substitute the phrase "Your good gifts"
with the fruit of the Spirit as found in
Galatians 5:22–23. Sing "love and joy,"
"peace and patience," "kindness too,"
"goodness too," "faithfulness," and
"self-control."

The Trinity

We Praise the Holy Trinity

Melody: *Three Jolly Fishermen*

We praise the Holy Trinity.
We praise the Holy Trinity.
Father, Son, and Holy Ghost,
Father, Son, and Holy Ghost,
We praise the Holy Trinity.

Praise the Holy Trinity

Melody: *Jesus Loves Me*

Praise the Holy Trinity,
Three-in-One and One-in-Three.
Father, Son, and Holy Ghost
Name the God we love the most.
Let us sing praises,
Let us sing praises,
Let us sing praises
Unto the Trinity.

We Believe in One True God

Melody: *Do-Re-Me*

We believe in one true God.
Praise the Holy Trinity.
To God's holy name we sing,
Join the praise of heaven's host.
God, our Father, made all things.
Jesus died for all our sins.
His Spirit helps us in our need.
Praise the Holy Trinity.

Holy, Holy, Holy Lord

Melody: *Yankee Doodle*

Holy, holy, holy Lord,
Oh, Lord of Hosts, we praise You.
Your glory fills both heaven and earth.
We sing our praises to You.

Holy, holy, holy Lord,
Father, Son, and Spirit,
Your glory fills both heaven and earth.
We sing our praises to You.

I Know That God the Father Made Me

Melody: *I Have Decided to Follow Jesus*

I know that God the Father made me,
I know that God the Father made me,
I know that God the Father made me.
God loves me so. God loves me so.

I know that Jesus has died to save me,
I know that Jesus has died to save me,
I know that Jesus has died to save me.
God loves me so. God loves me so.

I know the Spirit now lives within me,
I know the Spirit now lives within me,
I know the Spirit now lives within me.
God loves me so. God loves me so.

I praise and thank my God forever,
I praise and thank my God forever,
I praise and thank my God forever.
God loves me so. God loves me so.

Give Praise to God the Father

Melody: *My Hat, It Has Three Corners*

Give praise to God the Father,
Give praise to God the Son,
And to the Holy Spirit,
Now let our praise be sung.

Glory to the Trinity

Melody: *Yankee Doodle*

Glory to the Trinity.
Glory to the Father.
Glory to the Son and Spirit,
Praise God's name forever.

Baptism

I Thank God

Melody: *Mary Had a Little Lamb*

I thank God I was baptized,
Was baptized, was baptized.
I thank God I was baptized,
Into His family.

I thank God that to my heart,
To my heart, to my heart,
I thank God that to my heart
The Holy Spirit came.

I thank God that all my sins,
All my sins, all my sins,
I thank God that all my sins,
By grace, were washed away.

I thank God for giving me,
Giving me, giving me,
I thank God for giving me
The gift of faith that day.

Jesus Was Baptized by John

Melody: *Mary Had a Little Lamb*

When Jesus was baptized by John,
Baptized by John, baptized by John.
The Holy Spirit, like a dove,
Came down for all to see.

God the Father spoke that day,
Spoke that day, spoke that day.
"This is My Son," He then said.
"In Him I am well pleased."

I am baptized in God's name,
In God's name, in God's name.
I am baptized in God's name.
I am now God's own child.

25

I Am Baptized

Melody: *Sailing, Sailing*

I am baptized
Into God's family.
I now have become
   God's own dear child,
My sins are washed away.
Into my heart
With gifts of His grace and love,
The Holy Spirit comes to give
Me faith in God above.

On the Day
I Was Baptized

Melody: *B-I-N-G-O*

On the day I was baptized,
God's Holy Spirit came and
Made me God's dear child,
Made me God's dear child,
Made me God's dear child,
The Holy Spirit came.

Praise and Thanksgiving

Come and Worship God with Me

Melody: *Polly, Put the Kettle On*

Come and worship God with me;
Come and worship God with me;
Come and worship God with me;
Worship the Lord.

Come and Sing

Melody: *Jack and Jill*

Come and sing to God, our King.
And praise His name forever.
Day by day we praise His name
And worship Him forever.

Let us sing, "Great is the Lord,"
And praise His name forever.
Let us tell His mighty deeds
And worship Him forever.

Let's Give the Lord Our Praise

Melody: *The Hokey-Pokey*

Let's give the Lord our praise.
Hold out hands.

Let's give the Lord our prayers.
Hold up hands.

Let's give the Lord our thanks
Fold hands.

For all He does for us.
Clap hands.

Let's thank Him for His love.
Hold up hands.

Now every girl and boy,
Point around group.

Worship the Lord above.
Clap hands.

We Praise the Lord

Melody: *Clementine*

> Let us praise God,
> *Hold hands up.*
>
> Let us praise God,
> Let us praise our God today.
> Let us thank God,
> *Fold hand.*
>
> Let us thank God,
> Let us thank our God today.

Praise the Lord Now

Melody: *Alouette*

> Praise the Lord now,
> Everyone now praise Him.
> Praise the Lord
> Who has made everything.
>
> Praise the Lord now,
> Everyone now praise Him.
> Praise the Lord
> Who has made everything.
>
> Land and sky and sun and stars.
> Land and sky and sun and stars.
> Praise the Lord! Praise the Lord!
> Praise the Lord now!
>
> Praise the Lord now,
> Everyone now praise Him.
> Praise the Lord
> Who has made everything.

Repeat, substituting new phrases for "Land and sky and sun and stars." Repeat all the phrases each time you sing a new stanza.

28

Creation

God Made Everything

Melody: *The Farmer in the Dell*

> God made everything.
> God made everything.
> God made _____
> and _____.
> God made everything.

Have the children fill in the blanks with the names of things God has made such as birds, and plants, and animals.

God Made Everything We See

Melody: *Mulberry Bush*

> God made everything we see,
> Animals, birds, and the deep blue sea,
> Land, and plants, and the sky so blue.
> And He made people too.

If You're Happy That God Made You

Melody: *If You're Happy*

> If you're happy that God made you,
> Clap your hands. *Clap, clap.*
> If you're happy that God made you,
> Clap your hands. *Clap, clap.*
> If you're happy that God made you,
> Let your happiness shine through you.
> If you're happy that God made you,
> Clap your hands. *Clap, clap.*

> If you're happy that God made you,
> Stomp your feet. *Stomp, stomp …*

> If you happy that God made you,
> Shout your praise, *"Praise the Lord!"* …

> If you're happy that God made you,
> Do all three—
> *Clap, clap, stomp, stomp, "Praise the Lord!"*

Our Savior

Who Is Jesus?

Melody: *Are You Sleeping?*

Who is Jesus? Who is Jesus?
He's God's Son. He's God Son.
Born to be our Savior,
Born to be our Savior.
Follow Him. Follow Him.

I'm a Little Christian

Melody: *I'm a Little Teapot*

I'm a little Christian, saved and free.
Jesus came to die for me.
He is always with me, every day.
He will hear me when I pray.

Jesus Loves Me

Melody: *Clementine*

Jesus loves me, Jesus loves me.
He takes care of me each day.
He is always there beside me.
He takes care of me each day.

Come, Follow

Melody: *Twinkle, Twinkle Little Star*

Jesus calls, "Come, follow Me,
Follow, follow, follow Me."
We will follow, yesiree,
When Jesus calls, "Come, follow Me."
Jesus calls, "Come, follow Me,
Follow, follow, follow Me."

Where Is Jesus?

Melody: *Are You Sleeping?*

Where is Jesus? Where is Jesus?
  Hold hands out.

Everywhere, everywhere.
  Point all around.

He will watch and keep me,
  Point to self.

He will watch and keep me,
In His care, in His care.
  Fold hands in prayer.

Forgiveness

I Am Justified by Faith

Melody: *Michael, Row the Boat Ashore*

I am justified by faith.
Alleluia!
Not by works, but by God's grace.
Alleluia!
I will not boast of earning heaven.
Alleluia!
God's free gift is our salvation.
Alleluia!

Forgiveness Is a Gift

Melody: *The Old Gray Mare*

Forgiveness is a gift of the Lord to me,
Gift of the Lord to me,
Gift of the Lord to me.
Forgiveness is a gift of the Lord to me,
A gift of grace so free.

I'm Forgiven, I'm Forgiven

Melody: *This Old Man*

I'm forgiven, I'm forgiven.
On the cross Christ died for me.
From sin and death, I now have been
    set free.
On the cross Christ died for me.

Jesus Died upon the Cross

Melody: *Jack and Jill*

Jesus died upon the cross
To win for us salvation.
Jesus died to set us free
So we can live forgiven.

*Take time to explain the meaning of
"salvation" if used with young children.*

31

Forgiveness Comes as a Gift

Melody: *Where, Oh, Where Has My Little Dog Gone?*

Forgiveness comes as a gift from the Lord.
Christ died on the cross for our sins.
From the power of sin we have now been set free.
Christ died for you and for me.

God's Love and Care

My Help Comes

Melody: *Michael, Row the Boat Ashore*

My help comes from God above,
Alleluia!
He who made me with His love.
Alleluia!

He who made all that I see.
Alleluia!
Ever loves and stays by me.
Alleluia!

1, 2, 3 Great Blessings

Melody: *Ten Little Indians*

1 great, 2 great, 3 great blessings,
4 great, 5 great, 6 great blessings.
Many blessings, without number
Come from God each day.

Our God Is with Us

Melody: *Auld Lang Syne*

Our God is with us every day,
He is with us all the time.
At home, at school, at work, at play;
God is with us all the time.

The Love of God

Melody: *The Wheels on the Bus*

The love of God goes on and on,
On and on,
On and on.
The love of God goes on and on.
He loves us without end.

God Loves Us

Melody: *Three Blind Mice*

God is love. God is love.
Point up.

God loves you. God loves me.
Point to others, then self.

God loved us so much
that He sent His own Son,
Pretend to rock baby.

Who died on the cross
to forgive everyone.
Make cross with fingers.

God is love. God is love.
Point up.

I Know God Chose Me

Melody: *I Have Decided to Follow Jesus*

I know God chose me to be His child.
I know God chose me to be His child.
I know God chose me to be His child.
God loves me so. God loves me so.

I live in God's grace, now and forever.
I live in God's grace, now and forever.
I live in God's grace, now and forever.
God loves me so. God loves me so.

I thank my God for His love and favor.
I thank my God for His love and favor.
I thank my God for His love and favor.
God loves me so. God loves me so.

As a Father Has Compassion

Melody: *Did You Ever See a Lassie?*

As a father has compassion,
Compassion, compassion;
As a father has compassion
Upon his children;
So the Lord will have compassion,
Compassion, compassion;
So the Lord will have compassion
On those that He loves.

*Explain the meaning of the word
"compassion" before using with small
children.*

Blessed Be the Lord, My Rock

Melody: *Jack and Jill*

Blessed be the Lord, my rock,
He's always there beside me.
God's my tower, He's my shield.
He's always there beside me.

I Am Loved by God Above

Melody: *I Am Jesus' Little Lamb*

I am blessed by God above,
He surrounds me with His love.
By Christ's death I am forgiven.
Life eternal, I am given.
As God's child I now can rest,
By His grace forever blest.

Sing a Song

Melody: *Sing a Song of Sixpence*

Sing a song of God's love,
Love that has no end.
Love that sent a Savior
To save us from our sin.
Sing a song of God's love,
A love that's everywhere.
Love that's any place we go,
It's always, always there.

The Christian Life

Jesus' Love

Melody: *Jingle Bells*

Jesus' love, Jesus' love,
Helps us every day,
Helps us do the things we should,
Helps us learn to pray.

Jesus' love, Jesus' love,
Helps us to learn to share,
Helps us to grow in His love,
Helps us learn to care.

Jesus' love, Jesus' love,
Helps us to forgive,
Helps us love as we are loved,
Helps us learn to give.

You Can Share

Melody: *Did You Ever See a Lassie?*

You can share God's love with others,
With others, with others.
You can share God's love with others,
With all that you meet.
With father and mother,
With sister and brother,
You can share God's love with others,
With all that you meet.

Have children substitute names of other people with whom they can share God's love. Example: "With teachers and classmates" or "With aunts and with uncles."

What a Blessing

Melody: *Clementine*

What a blessing,
What a blessing,
What a blessing I can be.
When God's Spirit
Lives within me,
What a blessing I can be.

I can serve God,
I can serve God,
I can serve God every day.
When God's Spirit
Lives within me,
I can serve God every day.

I can show love,
I can show love,
I can show love every day.
When God's Spirit
Lives within me,
I can show love every day.

Show God's Love

Melody: *Skip to My Lou*

Show God's love in all you do.
Show God's love in all you do.
Show God's love in all you do.
In what you say and what you do.

Show God's love in all you say.
Show God's love in all you say.
Show God's love in all you say.
In what you do and what you say.

Oh, Be Joyful

Melody: *Clementine*

Oh, be joyful. Oh, be joyful.
Oh, be joyful every day.
Don't stop praying;
"Thanks" keep saying.
Oh, be joyful every day.

God's Helpers

Melody: *Mulberry Bush*

This is the way the organist plays,
  Play the organ.
Organist plays, organist plays.
This is the way the organist plays,
Every Sunday morning.

This is the way the choir sings ...
  Hold music and sing.

This is the way the pastor preaches ...
  Extend hands out.

This is the way the people pray ...
  Fold hands.

This is the way the children sing ...
  Hold music and sing.

This is the way the ushers help ...
  Pretend to pass out bulletins or
help people.

This is the way the greeters smile ...
  Smile and nod head.

This is the way the bell choir plays ...
  Play bells.

*Continue with other helpers found in
your own worship service.*

Jesus Helps Us Love Each Other

Melody: *London Bridge*

Jesus helps us love each other,
Love each other, love each other.
Jesus helps us love each other,
Jesus helps us.

Jesus hears us when we pray,
When we pray, when we pray.
Jesus hears us when we pray,
Jesus hears us.

Come and Follow

Melody: *Ten Little Indians*

Jesus says to come and follow,
Jesus says to come and follow,
Jesus says to come and follow,
Come and follow Him.

Jesus helps us come and follow,
Jesus helps us come and follow,
Jesus helps us come and follow,
Come and follow Him.

Prayer

O God, Our Lord

Melody: *Our God, Our Help in Ages Past*

O Mighty God, who loves us so,
To you we come today.
O Savior, hear and help us now,
As we our prayers shall say.

Use as an opening to a group prayer in which children are invited to add individual prayers.

Call upon Me

Melody: *Skip to My Lou*

Call upon Me in the day of trouble,
Call upon Me in the day of trouble,
Call upon Me in the day of trouble
And I will deliver you.

Heavenly Father, Who Has Said

Melody: *Jesus Loves Me*

Heavenly Father, Who has said
You will hear us when we pray.
Trusting in Your Word we come.
You will hear the words we say.
Lord, hear our prayer now.
Lord, hear our prayer now.

For _____

and _____

Insert specific names of children.

Lord, hear our prayer today.

Ask and It Will

Melody: *God Is So Good*

Ask and it will,
Ask and it will,
Ask and it will
Be given unto you.

Seek and you'll find,
Seek and you'll find,
Knock and the door will
Be opened unto you.

Pray to the Lord,
Pray to the Lord,
Pray to the Lord
And He will hear you pray.

I Love to Worship and Sing Praise

Melody: *Happy Wanderer*
(*I Love to Go a' Wandering*)

I love to worship and sing praise
Unto the Lord above.
And as I sing, I thank the Lord
For all His gifts of love.

Refrain:
Thank the Lord.
Thank the Lord.
Thank the Lord for He is good.
Thank the Lord.
Thank the Lord.
Thank the Lord for He is good.

When the Morning Sun

Melody: *Mulberry Bush*

When the morning sun comes up,
Sun comes up, sun comes up,
When the morning sun comes up,
Pray to God with joy.

When the evening sun goes down,
Sun goes down, sun goes down,
When the evening sun goes down,
Pray to God with joy.

Our God Will Hear Us Every Day

Melody: *Auld Lang Syne*

Our God will hear us when we pray,
He will hear all that we say.
He's there to help us day and night,
With His power and great might.

Father, Hear the Prayer

Melody: *Row, Row, Row Your Boat*

Father, hear the prayer
That Your children say.
Forgive the sins that we've done
  wrong.
Keep us safe this day.

Pray to God

Melody: *Jingle Bells*

Pray to God,
Pray to God,
Pray to God each day.
He will hear
All that you say.
Pray to God each day.

The Lord's Prayer

Melody: *Our God, Our Help in Ages Past*

Our Heavenly Father, hear our prayer,
Most holy be Your name.
Your kingdom come. Your will be done
In heaven and earth the same.

Give us today our daily bread.
Forgive our sins today,
As we forgive those who have sinned
Against us, Lord we pray.

And all that leads us to do wrong,
Keep far from us today.
Deliver us from evil's power.
Lord, keep us safe, we pray.

For You are King of everything,
With power and glory too.
We trust that now and for all time,
There's nothing You can't do.

Give Thanks unto the Lord

Melody: *The Farmer in the Dell*

Give thanks unto the Lord.
Give thanks unto the Lord.
Oh, thank the Lord
For He is good.
Give thanks unto the Lord.

Oh, Give Thanks

Melody: *Johnny Appleseed Song*

O-h, the Lord is good to me,
My thanks I give to Him,
For all the things He gives to me,

the _____,

the _____,

and the _____.
The Lord is good to me.
Amen, amen,
In Jesus' name. Amen.
A-men.

Fill in the blanks with names of specific things for which you want to thank God.

Oh, Give Thanks

Melody: *Happy Birthday*

Oh, give thanks to the Lord,
For He is so good.
His mercy is forever.
Give thanks to the Lord.

Jesus, Come

Melody: *This Old Man*

> Jesus, come,
> Be our guest.
> May Your gifts to us be blest.
> For everything You give to us this day.
> A prayer of thanks we now will say.

Come, Lord Jesus

Melody: *Row, Row, Row Your Boat*

> Come, come, come, dear Lord,
> Come and be our guest.
> May all the blessings that You give
> Be to us now blest.

We Give God Thanks

Melody: *Auld Lang Syne*

> We thank You, God, for all our food,
> For all You give to us.
> In Jesus' name, we give our thanks
> For all You give to us.

Let children substitute names of specific foods in the second and fourth lines.

Evangelism

Oh, Where

Melody: *Where, Oh, Where Has My Little Dog Gone?*

Oh, where, oh, where,
Can you share the Good News
Of Jesus and His great love?
Everywhere and anywhere you may go,
Share the news of His love.

Share the Good News

Melody: *Clementine*

Share the Good News,
Share the Good News,
Share the Good News
Of God's love.
Jesus died for everybody.
Share the Good News
Of God's love.

We've Got a Job

Melody: *This Is the Day*

We've got a job,
We've got a job
To do for the Lord,
To do for the Lord.
Our job's to tell,
Our job's to tell,
Of Jesus' love for all
Of Jesus' love for all.
Share the Good News with ev'ryone
    you know.
Spread the Good News everywhere
    that you go.
We've got a job,
We've got a job
To do for the Lord.

Spread the News

Melody: *Row, Row, Row Your Boat*

Spread, spread, spread the news
Of Jesus and His love.
At home, at school, at play each day
Tell of Jesus' love.

Have children substitute the names of other places where they can share the story of Jesus and His love.

You Can Tell

Melody: *London Bridge*

You can tell of Jesus' love,
Jesus' love, Jesus' love.
You can tell of Jesus' love
To everybody.

You can say, "He died for you,
Died for you, died for you."
You can say, "He died for you,
For everybody."

Jesus' Love Is for Everyone

Melody: *The Wheels on the Bus*

The love of God is for everyone,
Everyone, everyone.
The love of God is for everyone
All around the world.

Go, spread the news of Jesus' love,
Jesus' love, Jesus' love.
Go, spread the news of Jesus' love
All around the world.

If You Have Good News to Share

Melody: *If You're Happy*

If you have Good News to share,
Then you can tell. *Clap, clap.*
If you have Good News to share,
Then you can tell. *Clap, clap.*
If you have Good News to share,
Tell about it everywhere.
If you have Good News to share,
Then you can tell. *Clap, clap.*

If you know of Jesus' love,
Then you can tell. *Stomp, stomp.*
If you know of Jesus' love,
Then you can tell. *Stomp, stomp.*
If you know of Jesus' love,
Tell about it everywhere.
If you know of Jesus' love,
Then you can tell. *Stomp, stomp.*

All around the Wonderful World

Melody: *Pop! Goes the Weasel*

All around this wonderful world,
God's people tell the story,
How Jesus died to save everyone.
I can tell the story!

Take turns singing the stanza, with different children popping up on the last line to sing, "I can tell the story."

God's Word

In the Bible

Melody: *Clementine*

In the Bible, in the Bible,
Make Bible book with hands and pretend to read.
In the Bible we can read
Of God's love in sending Jesus,
Make cross with fingers.
How He died for you and me.
Point to each other.

I Read in God's Word

Melody: *Happy Birthday*

I can read in God's Word
Pretend to read Bible.
That Jesus loves you.
Point to others.
Then I read in God's Word
Pretend to read Bible.
That Jesus loves me.
Point to self.

Read in God's Word

Melody: *Oh, When the Saints*

Read in God's Word,
Read in God's Word,
Read in the B-I-B-L-E.
Read the Good News that
Jesus loves you
In the B-I-B-L-E.

Substitute other things that you read in the Bible for the phrase "that Jesus loves you."

Old Testament Stories

Abraham

Melody: *This Old Man*

This old man, Abraham,
Left his home at God's command.
Then away he went with Sarah,
   his wife.
Off to start a brand new life.

This old man, Abraham,
Looked up at the stars at hand.
Then he heard God tell of children
   yet to come,
And of a special Promised One.

Jacob, Jacob

Melody: *Reuben and Rachel*

Jacob, Jacob, what did you dream
As you slept upon the ground?
"Of a stairway into heaven,
Angels climbed it up-and-down."

Jacob, Jacob, what did you dream,
On your pillow made of stone?
"That the Lord Himself would
   keep me
Safe and sound till I came home."

The Birth of Isaac

Melody: *John Brown's Baby*

Abraham and Sarah had a bouncing baby boy.
   Bounce baby on knee.
Abraham and Sarah had a bouncing baby boy.
Abraham and Sarah had a bouncing baby boy,
And Isaac was his name.

Abraham and Sarah had a laughing baby boy.
   Hold hand over mouth as if laughing.
Abraham and Sarah had a laughing baby boy.
Abraham and Sarah had a laughing baby boy,
And Isaac was his name.

Abraham and Sarah loved their bouncing baby boy.
   Hug bouncing baby.
Abraham and Sarah loved their bouncing, baby boy.
Abraham and Sarah loved their bouncing, baby boy,
And thanked the Lord for him.

Sleep, Baby Moses

Melody: *Rock-a-bye Baby*

Sleep, baby Moses,
   Rock baby.
Gently you float.
Miriam is watching
Your small basket-boat.
You're not alone,
For God from above
Is also there keeping
You safe in His love.

Sleep, baby Moses
   Rock baby.
In your basket-bed.
God's holy angels
Watch by your head.
You're not alone,
For God from above
Is also there keeping
You safe in His love.

Moses

Melody: *B-I-N-G-O*

Miriam watched the baby boy
Floating in the river.
M-O-S-E-S,
M-O-S-E-S,
M-O-S-E-S,
Moses was his name-o!

A princes found the baby boy
Floating in the river.
M-O-S-E-S,
M-O-S-E-S,
M-O-S-E-S,
Moses was his name-o!

The baby grew to be a man,
Called to be God's helper.
M-O-S-E-S,
M-O-S-E-S,
M-O-S-E-S,
And Moses was his name-o!

Moses Went up on the Mountain

Melody: *The Bear Went over the Mountain*

Moses went up on the mountain,
Moses went up on the mountain,
Moses went up on the mountain,
The Lord, his God, to see.
The Lord, his God, to see.
The Lord, his God, to see.
Moses went up on the mountain,
Moses went up on the mountain,
Moses went up on the mountain,
The Lord, his God, to see.

(Optional: Moses went up on Mt. Sinai)

Then God gave the Ten
    Commandments,
God gave the Ten Commandments,
God gave the Ten Commandments,
On two tablets of stone.
On two tablets of stone.
On two tablets of stone.
God gave the Ten Commandments,
God gave the Ten Commandments,
God gave the Ten Commandments,
On two tablets of stone.

Ten Commandments

Melody: *Ten Little Indians*

One, and two, and three
Commandments,
Four, and five, and six
Commandments,
Seven, and eight, and nine
Commandments,
God gave Ten Commandments.

Old King David

Melody: *Old King Cole*

Old King David was a God-fearing soul,
And a God-fearing soul was he.
He wrote the Psalms in praise of God.
And he planned for God's temple-to-be.

God's People Go Marching

Melody: *The Ants Go Marching*

God's people go marching one by one. Hurrah! Hurrah!
God's people go marching one by one. Hurrah! Hurrah!
God's people go marching one by one,
A little one stops to sit in the sun.
And they all go marching through the Red Sea on their way to the Promised Land.

God's people go marching two by two. Hurrah! Hurrah!
God's people go marching two by two. Hurrah! Hurrah!
God's people go marching two by two,
A little one stops to hear a cow moo.
And they all go marching through the Red Sea on their way to the Promised Land.

God's people go marching three by three. Hurrah! Hurrah!
God's people go marching three by three. Hurrah! Hurrah!
God's people go marching three by three,
A little one stops to look up at the sea.
And they all go marching through the Red Sea on their way to the Promised Land.

God's people go marching four by four. Hurrah! Hurrah!
God's people go marching four by four. Hurrah! Hurrah!
God's people go marching four by four,
A little one stops to play by the shore.
And they all go marching through the Red Sea on their way to the Promised Land.

God's people go marching five by five. Hurrah! Hurrah!
God's people go marching five by five. Hurrah! Hurrah!
God's people go marching five by five,
A little one stops to thank God he's alive.
And they all go marching through the Red Sea on their way to the Promised Land.

God's people go marching six by six. Hurrah! Hurrah!
God's people go marching six by six. Hurrah! Hurrah!
God's people go marching six by six,
A little one stops to throw some sticks.
And they all go marching through the Red Sea on their way to the Promised Land.

God's people go marching seven by seven. Hurrah! Hurrah!
God's people go marching seven by seven. Hurrah! Hurrah!
God's people go marching seven by seven,
A little one stops to look up to heaven.
And they all go marching through the Red Sea on their way to the Promised Land.

God's people go marching eight by eight. Hurrah! Hurrah!
God's people go marching eight by eight, Hurrah! Hurrah!
God's people go marching eight by eight,
A little one runs so he won't be late.
And they all go marching through the Red Sea on their way to the Promised Land.

God's people go marching nine by nine. Hurrah! Hurrah!
God's people go marching nine by nine. Hurrah! Hurrah!
God's people go marching nine by nine,
A little one stops and slows down the line.
And they all go marching through the Red Sea on their way to the Promised Land.

God's people go marching ten by ten. Hurrah! Hurrah!
God's people go marching ten by ten. Hurrah! Hurrah!
God's people go marching ten by ten,
A little one carefully carries his hen.
And they all go marching through the Red Sea on their way to the Promised Land.

New Testament Stories

There Were Four Jolly Fishermen

Melody: *Three Jolly Fishermen*

There were four jolly fishermen.
There were four jolly fisherman,
Peter, Andrew, James, and John.
Peter, Andrew, James, and John,
There were four jolly fishermen.

Jesus said, "Come, follow Me."
Jesus said, "Come, follow Me,
Peter, Andrew, James, and John."
Peter, Andrew, James, and John
Left their nets and followed Him.

Jesus says, "Come, follow Me."
Jesus says, "Come, follow Me,

_____
_____
_____
_____."
        Insert names of children.
Jesus says, "Come, follow Me."

Found a Savior

Melody: *Clementine*

"Found the Savior,
    Found the Savior,
    Found the Savior,"
    Philip said.
"Come and meet Him,
    Come and meet Him,
    Come and meet Him,"
    Philip said.

"Found the Savior,
    Found the Savior,
    Found the Savior,"
    We can say.
"Come and meet Him,
    Come and meet Him,
    Come and meet Him,"
    We can say.

Feeding of the Five Thousand

Melody: *There's a Hole in the Bucket*

"Where, oh, where shall we find bread?"
Said the disciples.
"Where, oh, where shall we find bread
For people to eat?"

"It would take so much money,"
Said Philip, said Philip.
"It would take so much money
To buy bread to eat."

"Here's a boy with five small loaves,"
Said Andrew, said Andrew.
"Here's a boy with five small loaves,
And two little fish."

"Tell the people to sit down,"
Said Jesus, said Jesus.
"Tell the people to sit down,
To sit down and eat."

Jesus gave thanks to God
For the loaves and the fishes.
Jesus gave thanks to God
For the loaves and the fish.

The food fed five thousand,
Five thousand, five thousand.
The food fed five thousand,
With twelve baskets left.

We know we can trust You,
Dear Jesus, dear Jesus.
We know we can trust You
To feed us each day.

Baa, Baa, Little Lamb

Melody: *Baa, Baa, Black Sheep*

Leader: Baa, baa, little lamb
Did you lose your way?
Sheep: Yes, sir. Yes, sir,
I was lost today.
Far from my shepherd,
Far from my home.
Far from my flock,
I ran off alone.
Leader: Baa, baa, little lamb,
Did you lose your way?
Sheep: Yes, sir. Yes, sir,
I was lost today.

Leader: Baa, baa, little lamb,
Who found you?
Sheep: My Good Shepherd,
Who loves you too.
Left His flock of ninety-nine.
Looked for me with love so kind.
Leader: Baa, baa, little lamb,
Your Shepherd looked for you?
Sheep: Yes, sir. Yes, sir,
And He found me too.

Leader: Dear little children,
Does your Shepherd love you?
Children: Yes, sir. Yes, sir,
He loves you too.
If we sin and go from Him,
Jesus brings us back to Him.
Leader: Dear little children,
Your Shepherd loves you.
Children: Yes, sir, yes, sir,
And He loves you too.

In a Boat upon the Sea

Melody: *Little Cabin in the Wood*

On the sea, calm as could be,
Jesus' friends sailed,
    happy as could be.
Suddenly a wind came up,
And they were filled with fear.
"It's a ghost!" they quickly cried,
As to them the Lord came near.
"It is I," Jesus told them,
"Do not be afraid."

The Wind Blew

Melody: *Rise and Shine*

The wind blew, the waves splashed,
The small boat was shaking, shaking.
The wind blew, the waves splashed,
The small boat was shaking, shaking.
Jesus' friends were quaking, quaking,
    quaking,
Quaking from their fear.

They went and woke Jesus
Who had been sleeping, sleeping.
Went and woke Jesus
Who had been sleeping, sleeping.
Said, "Lord, save us now
    from sinking, sinking
Deep into the sea."

"Be quiet," said Jesus,
Unto the windy, windy.
"Be quiet," said Jesus,
Unto the windy, windy.
At His word then all the stormy,
    stormy
Stopped and became still.

Jesus Calls Matthew

Melody: *I've Been Working on the Railroad*

Matthew was a tax collector
All the live-long day.
Matthew sat collecting taxes
When Jesus came that way.
Jesus stopped to talk to Matthew.
"Follow me," He said.
Matthew rose and followed Jesus,
Followed where He led.

Refrain:

"Come and follow Me,
Come and follow Me."
Jesus says to us today,
"Come and follow Me,
Come and follow Me."
Jesus says to us today.

Peter, Peter, What Do You Think?

Melody: *Reuben and Rachel*

Jesus: Peter, Peter, what do you think?
Who do people say I am?

Peter: You are Christ, the promised Savior,
The Son of the living God.

Teacher: Children, children, what do you think?
Who is Jesus, whom you love?

Children: He is Christ, the promised Savior,
The Son of the living God.

Have different children sing different parts.

Saul Becomes Paul

Melody: *This Old Man*

A man named Saul
Went the way
To Damascus one fine day,
Whe-en in a bright light
Jesus spoke to Saul,
And changed him to
The Apostle Paul.

Philip and the Man in the Chariot

Melody: *Where, Oh, Where Has My Little Dog Gone?*

What, oh, what do these Bible words say?
Oh, what, oh, what can they mean?
A man in a chariot thought one day.
What, oh, what can they mean?

A man named Philip appeared to the man.
From God to the man he was sent.
Philip then rode with the man on his way,
Telling what the Bible words meant.

The man was happy to hear Phillip tell
What the Bible did say.
The man believed Jesus had died for his sin,
And asked to be baptized that day.

Welcome Song

Melody: *Are You Sleeping?*

Where is _____?
Where is _____?
Please stand up.
Please stand up.
We're so glad to see you.
We're so glad to see you.
God loves you!
God loves you!

Insert the name of a child.

Loved by the Lord

Melody: *Skip to My Lou*

_____ is loved by the Lord,
_____ is loved by the Lord,
_____ is loved by the Lord,

Jesus loves him/her very much.

Insert the name of a child.

In His Hands

Melody: *He's Got the Whole World
           in His Hands*

He's got everyone here in His hands.
He's got everyone here in His hands.
He's got everyone here in His hands.
He holds all of us in His hands.

He's got _____ and
_____ in His hands.

He's got _____ and
_____ in His hands.

He's got _____ and
_____ in His hands.

He holds all of us in His hands.

Insert children's names.

Closing

The Lord Bless You

Melody: *Clementine*

The Lord bless you.
The Lord keep you.
The Lord watch you from above.
The Lord's peace be with you always.
The Lord keep you in His love.

May God Bless and Keep You Always

Melody: *Row, Row, Row Your Boat*

May God bless you now,
As you go on your way.
May He look on you with love
And give you peace today.

The Lord Will Bless You

Melody: *Auld Lang Syne*

The Lord will bless you,
And will keep you safe upon your way.
The Lord will shine His face on you,
And give you peace today.

Jesus, Jesus

Melody: *Sailing, Sailing*

Jesus, Jesus, now bless us on our way.
Today and through the coming week,
Oh, keep us safe we pray.

Jesus, Jesus, now bless us on our way.
Help us to show what we have learned
In all we do and say.

May the Lord Bless You

Melody: *Beautiful Savior*

May the Lord bless you.
May the Lord keep you.
And may His face look upon you too.
May He give you His peace,
And may His countenance
Shine with His loving grace on you.

Offering

Offering Song

Melody: *It's Raining, It's Pouring*

We're bringing our offering
With praise and thanksgiving.
To God above and His great love,
A song of thanks we're singing.

Bless the Offering

Melody: *Mulberry Bush*

Bless our offerings, Lord, we pray,
Lord, we pray, Lord, we pray.
Bless our offerings, Lord, we pray,
That we bring You this day.

Bless the Gifts

Melody: *Yankee Doodle*

We bring these gifts to You today.
Take them, Lord, and bless them,
To help others in their need.
Oh, take them, Lord, and bless them.

We Bring Our Gifts to You, O Lord

Melody: *Jack and Jill*

We bring our gifts to You, O Lord,
In love and in thanksgiving.
We give what You first gave to us,
In love and in thanksgiving.

Thank You, Lord

Melody: *Three Blind Mice*

Thank You, Lord,
Thank You, Lord,
For Your gifts,
For Your gifts.
There's nothing we have
That does not come from You.
We give this as thanks
For all things that You do.
Our offering is given
In our love for You.
Thank You, Lord.
Thank You, Lord.

Birthday

Thank the Lord for Your Birthday

Melody: *Happy Birthday*

Thank the Lord for this day,
Thank the Lord for this day,
Thank the Lord for your birthday,
Thank the Lord for this day.

May Jesus Bless You

Melody: *Happy Birthday*

May Jesus bless you.
May Jesus bless you.
Bless you on your birthday,
May Jesus bless you.

God Bless You on Your Birthday

Melody: *The Bear Went over the Mountain*

God's blessings to you on your birthday.
God's blessings to you on your birthday.
God's blessings to you on your birthday,
God's blessings to you today.

God's blessings be to

_____ .

God's blessings be to

_____ .

God's blessings to you on your birthday.
God's blessings to you today.

Insert the name of a child.

Baptismal Birthday Song

Melody: *B-I-N-G-O*

When _____ was baptized,
    he/she was born
Again as God's dear child.
Today we thank the Lord,
Today we thank the Lord,
Today we thank the Lord,
On his/her baptismal birthday.

When _____ was baptized,
    all his/her sins
Were washed away that day.
Today we thank the Lord,
Today we thank the Lord,
Today we thank the Lord,
On his/her baptismal birthday.

Insert the name of the child.

Write Your Own Songs Here

Index